# I Wonder How Fish Sleep

Mona Gansberg Hodgson

Illustrated by
Chris Sharp

CPH®

SAINT LOUIS

*With love to Uncle Marvin and Aunt Marian.*
*Thanks for having such a fun place full of animals.*

## I Wonder Series

I Wonder Who Hung the Moon in the Sky
I Wonder Who Stretched the Giraffe's Neck
I Wonder How Fish Sleep

Text copyright © 1999 Mona Gansberg Hodgson
Art copyright © 1999 Concordia Publishing House
Published by Concordia Publishing House
3558 S. Jefferson Avenue, St. Louis, MO 63118-3968
Manufactured in the United States of America

1  2  3  4  5  6  7  8  9  10          08  07  06  05  04  03  02  01  00  99

The *I Wonder Series* will delight children while helping them grow in their understanding and appreciation of God. Readers will discover biblical truths through the experiences and whimsy of 7-year-old Jared.

This book, *I Wonder How Fish Sleep*, provides a playful exploration of how various creatures sleep and God's provision for us. The activities on pages 30–32 will help children apply and practice the truths revealed in Jared's imaginative investigation.

As you read this book together, share these Bible words with your child:

Give thanks to the LORD, for He is good; His love endures forever. *Psalm 107:1*

Enjoy!

*Mona Gansberg Hodgson*

Hi! My name is Jared. I live in Arizona.

Do you ever wonder about things? I do. Everything I see makes me wonder. I like to wonder. Do you like to wonder?

God made all the animals.
And God made you and me.
One day when I woke up early
to fish with Papa Ray, I began
to wonder.

How do animals sleep?
Do animals sleep like we do?
I wonder.

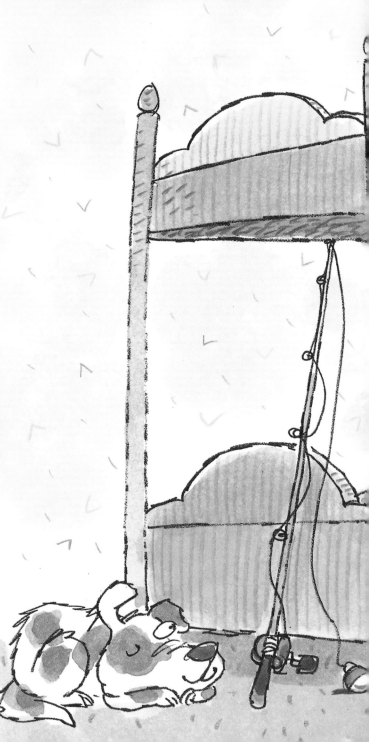

**I** sleep in my bedroom.

Where do skunks sleep?
I wonder.

Can you guess where
skunks sleep? Papa Ray says
skunks like to sleep in holes in
the ground. I'm glad I don't
have to sleep in the dirt.

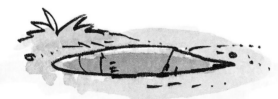

My mom and dad sleep on a water bed. Do you think fish sleep on a water bed? I wonder.

God made the oceans and the rivers where fish live. I think fish sleep IN a water bed.

It's too noisy around here.

I sleep on a bunk bed.
Do bats sleep on a bunk bed?
I wonder.

My mom says bats hang
upside down in a cave when
they nap.

I'm glad I don't have to
hang from my toes to doze.

Sometimes I sleep in a
sleeping bag. Do owls sleep in
sleeping bags? I wonder.

My dad says owls snooze
standing in a tree. I like the
way God made me. I'm glad I
don't have to balance on a
branch when I sleep.

**I** like to sleep on my side.

How do you think sea otters sleep? I wonder.

My book says sea otters sleep on their backs in the water. They roll themselves up in seaweed. That way the waves won't sweep them away while they slumber.

I like to curl up under my covers when I sleep. Do horses curl up under covers to sleep? I wonder.

My mom says horses like to sleep standing on their feet. I like the way God made me. I like to rest my feet when I sleep.

Feels Like Rain

Do you think turtles sleep with their heads on a pillow like I do? I wonder.

My dad says turtles don't need pillows. They tuck their heads into their shells when they sleep. Turtles really do tuck themselves in to sleep, don't they?

RACE TODAY

Papa Ray snores when he sleeps. Do you think dolphins snore when they sleep? I wonder.

Dolphins sleep under water. I think dolphins blow bubbles when they sleep. What do you think?

what's all the racket?

Do animals sleep at night like I do? I wonder.

My mom says God made some animals to be nocturnal. Nocturnal animals like to work and play in the moonlight. Koalas are nocturnal. They like to sleep in sunlight and eat lunch by moonlight.

24

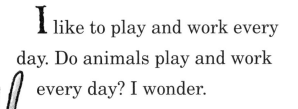

I like to play and work every day. Do animals play and work every day? I wonder.

Papa Ray says some animals hibernate. That means they sleep for a season. Some animals, like wood-chucks, sleep most of the winter when it's really cold.

How Much Wood Did He Chuck?

I like to wonder, don't you? When I wonder, I think about God. I like to think about God. I like to thank God for everything I have.

Give thanks to the LORD, for He is good; His love endures forever. *Psalm 107:1*

Thank You, God, for my bed, my pillow, and my covers.

Thank You, God, for taking care of everything I need.

Thank You for being my amazing God. I pray in the name of Jesus, my Savior.  Amen.

"Which of God's creatures do you wonder about? Tell me about them in the space below."